Basic Fly Casting

Fly fishing, I feel, is by far the most challenging and rewarding sport of all.

I enjoy it personally because there are so many skills to develop, so many places to go, and so many species to catch.

Hopefully, the Mastery Learning System will help you in sharing these feelings with me.

Doug Swisher

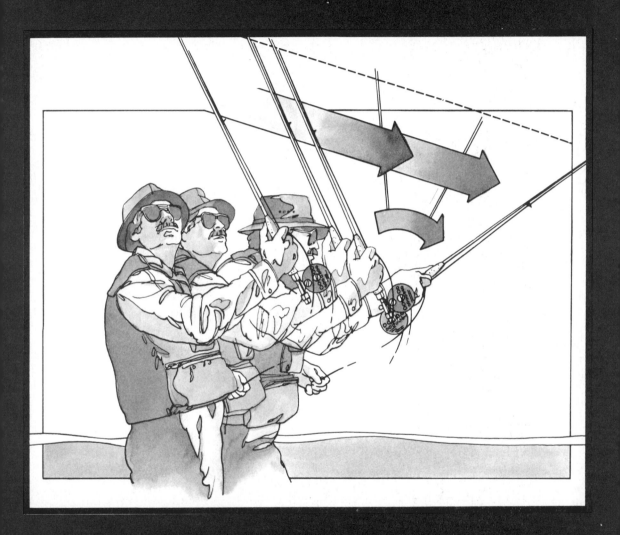

Basic Fly Casting

with

Doug Swisher

Trout Series
From Scientific Anglers

ISBN 0-9601424-3-6

Printed in the United States of America

Basic Fly Casting

Table of Contents

SECTION ONE:
HOW TO USE THIS MASTERY
VIDEO/GUIDEBOOK

SECTION TWO:
BASIC FLY CASTING

APPENDIX

I. What Is A Mastery Learning System?

The Fly Fishing for Trout Mastery Series is a complete body of knowledge from the most successful trout fishing authorities, each a skilled communicator. It's a collection of many *lifetimes* of knowledge compressed into just *hours* of video programs by our Mastery Learning System process. The benefit to you is that years of experience are refined into the concepts, principles and techniques which are the real *reasons* for experts high level of skill and success. These reasons are then transformed into a written and visual format designed for complete learning. It's exciting. Your progress will be fast because you won't have to guess and search for what you need to learn.

The learning system has two parts.

The visual format, the Mastery videotape, is designed so that you can see each scene and the action in it through the educated eyes of the expert. You see the action from the perspective of the expert. The same as if you were doing it yourself.

The second part of the learning system, the Mastery guidebook, further directs your attention to the critical specifics in each scene while pointing out when, how and why key concepts and principles are being used. The guidebook prevents you from becoming lost in the overall activity taking place in each scene. The result is a clearer focus on what is important.

All programs in the "Fly Fishing for Trout" series are designed for *progressive* development, each building on the next toward Mastery. There are three distinct stages of development in becoming a master trout fisherman: having the knowledge of what to do, being able to do it, and using your knowledge and ability to achieve new goals.

1. The Foundation Level Programs

Building your knowledge. We call this the *knowledge transfer* stage. Each program focuses on the essential concepts, guiding principles, their implications and critical relationships. All of which are necessary for you in order to understand the hows, whens and whys of the sport. Without your complete understanding of the foundation material, achieving Mastery is unlikely. These are *not* beginner programs. "Advanced" fishermen often find that they've "hit a wall" in their skill growth. Most often it's because they *thought* they had all the fundamentals "down cold," but they really did not. Their need is always the same - build a more complete and *stronger* foundation to support continued growth. Understanding, however, does not automatically guarantee you the ability to *apply* what you've learned. That's the *reason* for our Integration Programs, the second stage of your development toward Mastery.

2. The Integration Level Programs

Increasing your ability. This is the *ability transfer* stage, where your foundation knowledge metamorphoses into *increased success*. This stage shows you how to *apply* what you've learned from the Foundation Level Programs. Your performance skill will evolve from a conceptual understanding, not from just a list of steps or a series of tips. By watching the expert apply each concept and guiding principle in a typical fishing situation, you learn how, when and why they work. You will know what to do in any situation and know *why* it worked when you perfect the physical and mental skills shown in these programs. Now you're ready for the Challenge Level.

3. The Challenge Level Programs

Realization of your full potential. These programs are for the accomplished angler whose foundation and integration knowledge and skills have become second nature, subconscious, preparing them for the ultimate challenges of the sport, the final ascent to the Mastery stage. Each Challenge Level Program draws from your *new* complete foundation of knowledge and finely tuned skills to develop your own concepts and principles for mastery. The challenge programs will stimulate your continued skill growth, expanded involvement and increased satisfaction. Thus, the limiting factors for continued and greater success, whether your choice is to catch highly selective trout or giant steelhead, are only your imagination and physical ability.

Using These Materials In Combination

"Basic Fly Casting" consists of both a videotape and a guidebook. To transfer the most knowledge and ability, they are designed to be used together. The tape will enable you to see mastery in action, and the guidebook will focus your attention on specific points. Together the tape and guidebook are a learning *system*, developed for maximum ease of use and enjoyment of learning.

To receive the greatest value from these materials, we recommend you use them as follows:

1. View the whole tape - you are curious to see what's there, so go ahead. After you have an overview of what the tape covers, you will be ready to get into the subject and learn the concepts and techniques of fly casting.

2. Now, view the first segment of the tape, "Basic Fly Casting." Stop the tape, and turn to the guidebook while the tape is still fresh in your mind.

3. Read and study the first section of the guidebook. *Use* what you have learned.

4. Go back and review the same section of the video once again. Discover differences in what you see in the videotape the second time through compared to the first.

5. After you have completed the first section in this way, go do something else. Take a short break (at least 30 minutes) or even a long break (a day or more,) but take a break.

6. Use this "view-read-review-take-a-break" procedure for all segments of the program. If you use the materials in this way, you will get more insight into *why* your guide, Doug Swisher, is doing what he's doing. It is this insight that will help you to *own* the knowledge. When you *own* the material in this tape, your understanding will be automatic and instinctive, and you can apply

it to your situation more effectively than you could if you tried to follow Doug's procedure by rote. Knowing *why* you do something makes learning more fun, and more complete, because it truly puts you in *control*.

As you use these concepts, they will take on more complete meaning. Each time you view the videotape, you will hear additional information or see old information in new ways.

II. Introduction

"Basic Fly Casting" is one of the Foundation programs. It covers the fundamental principles and skills upon which advanced fly casting presentation techniques are based.

This program is designed to introduce you to the basic skills needed for successful fly fishing through the use of effective casting and presentation techniques.

As a Foundation program, the goal of "Basic Fly Casting" is for you to perfect the basic fly casting techniques, and the exercises that will help you acquire them. You will also be shown easy, effective ways to monitor your progress.

Nothing is more crucial to successful fly fishing than presentation. Someone else can show you where the fish are and select the proper fly for you, but it's up to you to present it correctly.

Effective presentation skill is not easy to learn. Beyond an understanding of fundamental casting principles, the best presentation teacher is practice. Only with devoted time and attention will you become a knowledgeable and successful fly caster. One half hour of practice, every day for two weeks, will yield impressive results.

With Doug Swisher's easy-to-learn, common sense approach, you will become familiar with the principle of straight-line energy transfer and see that successful fly casting has its foundation in this **straight-line principle.** You will learn to control all of your casting movements, from wrist to rod tip, so that they describe straight paths directly toward the target.

You will also become acquainted with the principle of **loop control.** By visually monitoring your line, and the loop that is created after it leaves the rod tip, you will learn how to achieve complete control of any cast. Understanding the visual aspect of fly casting and training your eye will accelerate learning and show you how to monitor your progress.

An "educated wrist" is the primary building block to developing your skills as a fly fisherman. You will be shown techniques that you can practice to help you achieve super-smooth, **"micro-second"** timing which will add power to your casting.

These fundamental skills will be applied to the basic casting stroke, upon which all presentation casts are based. Presentation casts range from the basic straight line and slack line casts, to the more complete and specialized casts that are covered in the next program, "Advanced Fly Casting."

Following Doug's system for mastering basic fly casting will maximize the quality of your fishing time and the fun of learning.

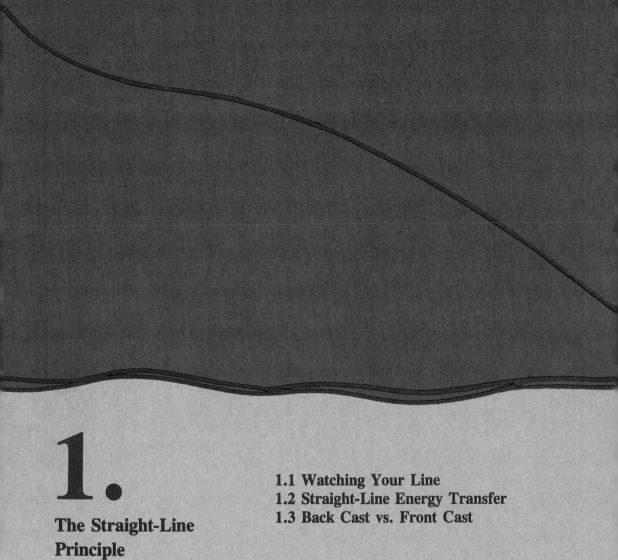

1.

The Straight-Line Principle

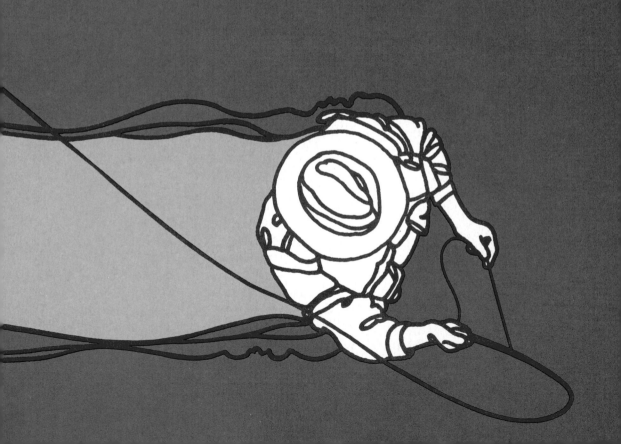

1.1 Watching Your Line

In order to learn the fine art of fly casting, it is necessary that you learn to see and recognize your mistakes. This can be done by paying careful and strict attention to watching the line.

FLY CASTING IS A VISUAL IMPROVEMENT SPORT. IT IS IMPOSSIBLE TO MAKE CORRECTIONS IF YOU CANNOT IDENTIFY YOUR MISTAKES.

The very best way to see exactly what you are doing, right or wrong, is to record yourself with a home videotape system. This will allow you to carefully analyze your every movement.

If videotaping yourself is not possible, you must carefully analyze your casting movements as you execute them. Then compare what you saw with how Doug does it on the tape.

Concentrating on your line and your body movement provides the all-important mental confidence that is crucial to successful fly fishing.

In order to see better, use a bright colored line both on the practice field and when actually fishing. Do not be concerned that a bright colored line will scare away fish. Bad casts scare fish - not bright line.

Counter Number

You will notice that Doug wears sunglasses when practicing outside, or while fishing. Sunglasses are an essential tool when you hit the water or practice field. For one thing, they offer your eyes protection from an errant fly, and for another, polarized lenses allow you to cut through the sun's glare on the water's surface. With them, you can see right into the water and have the advantage of actually seeing fish, instead of just "blind fishing."

At this point in developing your foundation casting skills, the best piece of equipment to use is a simple yarn rod. This useful tool can be easily constructed by threading a piece of large diameter, thick, brightly-colored "craft" yarn through the tip portion of any rod. The yarn rod can be used virtually anywhere, even in the comfort of your home.

Practice along with the video. The yarn rod is the tool that makes the Mastery System truly interactive between "visualizing" and "doing." The transfer of one ability to the other is simplified by being able to "do" a particular technique with your yarn rod as you "see" it on the videotape.

The yarn acts exactly like a real fly line, only in slow motion. The yarn's large diameter creates a great deal of wind resistance, slowing down its movement and making it easier to visualize what you are doing. This allows you to practice and perfect the new skills necessary to become a proficient fly caster. Also, your mistakes will be highly visible, standing out like a "sore thumb," thus allowing you to identify them quickly and then make the proper corrections.

Practicing with your yarn rod will not only be an invaluable aid in learning the basic casting stroke, but will also be most helpful in mastering the various presentation casts that you will be learning later in this tape and in the "Advanced Fly Casting" tape.

Whether on the practice field, on the water, or in your den at home, every moment that you spend practicing is "golden." Throughout this Mastery Series, you will improve your skills only with practice.

TO HELP YOU ACHIEVE MASTERY OF THE SPORT, THE LEARNING SYSTEM IS THE SAME FOR EVERY SKILL THAT YOU WILL NEED TO DEVELOP: TRAIN YOUR MIND TO RECOGNIZE THE RIGHT TECHNIQUE — AND THEN TRAIN YOUR MUSCLES TO DO IT.

In other types of casting, the lure's weight loads the rod, and the lure drags the almost weightless line behind it. In fly casting the roles are reversed. The weight is in the line, which loads the rod and drags the fly behind it. The flies

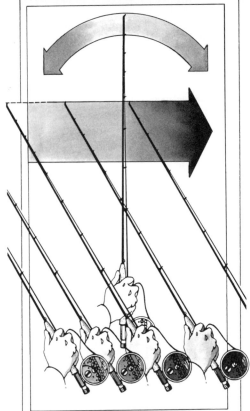

The straighter the movement of the rod tip, the tighter the loop. The more the rod tip arcs, or drops away from a straight line, the wider the loop.

you will use are so light, it would be impossible to cast them without the weight of the line.

1.2 Straight-Line Energy Transfer

The most important fly casting concept can be summed up into a single word - **straight.** In fly casting, you will be striving continually for relatively straight movements rather than movements that describe arcs. This basic concept of **straight-line energy transfer** is applied to almost every phase of fly casting.

Arcing Dissipates Energy In Too Many Directions

When you move the rod tip in an arcing or circular motion, you waste the power of your cast by dissipating its power in too many directions. A straight-line motion, on the other hand, concentrates all of the power in one direction in a straight, direct path toward the target. Notice that Doug drives his rod tip in as straight a line as possible.

Every Movement Of Your Casting Stroke Should Describe A Straight Line

Keep your eye on the tip of the rod. It will determine the direction of your cast.

The rod tip should not arc. It should move straight toward your target in a straight line on a flat plane.

Your Line Goes Where Your Rod Tip Goes.

To help you keep your rod tip moving in a perfectly straight path, pretend the very tip of your rod is attached to a clothesline or wire, or that it is in a straight track in the ceiling and your tip cannot get away from it.

Also, if your videotape player has such a feature, you can "freeze-frame" Doug's examples so that you can directly compare and analyze your technique with his at the push of a button.

Later in this guidebook, you will be introduced to the basic casting stroke. For now, we will concentrate on the separate elements that comprise the basic casting stroke, so that you will have carefully analyzed its elements before putting them all together on the practice field or on the water.

As you watch Doug on the videotape, pay close attention to his arm and wrist movements during his casts. The basic casting stroke is made up of arm and wrist movements. The arm "sets up" the cast and the wrist supplies the power of the cast. You need to have a clear mental picture of

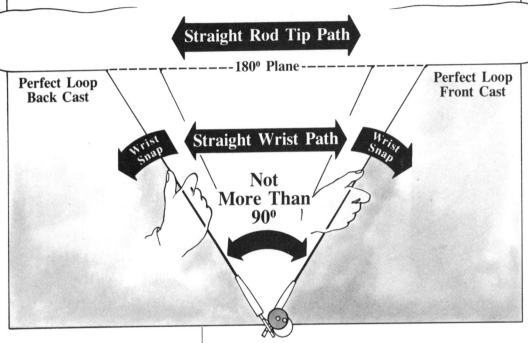

Straight Rod Tip Path

- - 180⁰ Plane - - - - -

Perfect Loop Back Cast

Perfect Loop Front Cast

Wrist Snap

Straight Wrist Path

Wrist Snap

Not More Than 90⁰

Although the Basic Casting Stroke is essentially one fluid movement, it is comprised of many separate body movements. Here we see the angles that these movements create and the planes on which they are drawn.

what a properly executed cast looks like *before* you can effectively train your muscles to perform the cast.

Both the arm and the wrist should move in as straight a line as possible. This ensures that the rod tip will move in a straight line. It is the combination of these separate movements into one fluid basic casting stroke that makes a successful caster.

1.3 Back Cast vs. Front Cast

Since every forward cast is preceded by a back cast, it is important to watch them both. Always watch your **front cast** *and* your **back cast.** Particular attention should be given to the back cast. This is the one that we are *not* used to watching, so it needs extra attention.

Stand slightly sideways so you can watch both casts comfortably.

Without A Good Back Cast, It Is Almost Impossible To Make A Good Front Cast.

The front and back casts should be in a perfectly straight line. As an aid, visualize an imaginary wire drawn tight between the two extreme points of your cast, and make sure that both your front and back casts "line up" on the wire. Better yet, whether you are practicing indoors or out, look for a straight reference line that can be "traced" by your rod tip during your casting stroke, and position yourself so that you can follow that reference line with your rod tip. Use a straight roof line, a telephone wire, or ceiling tiles to reference your straight-line movement.

Also, it is important for the line to be straight in one direction before you apply power in the other direction. A crooked line is very difficult

Find horizontal lines to trace visually with your rod tip.

to cast, while a straight line is easy to cast. This is another example where visualization is critical.

Learn To Be A "Line Watcher."

Remember that your entire arm and shoulder should contribute to the straight-line movement. By freeing the elbow, and allowing it to move back and forth, you'll find that it is much easier to make the rod tip travel along a perfectly straight line. When you lock your elbow to your side, forming a fixed pivotal point, you will find it very difficult to make the rod tip travel in a straight line.

Proper casting is *not* based on continuous, arcing movements, but instead, on stop and go, straight-line movements. The real key to good casting is not only developing a quick, smooth, micro-second wrist, but also teaching the wrist to snap straight at the target - not down. Envision a baseball pitcher who throws the ball straight to the batter - not down, so that he hits himself in the foot. Think straight-line, and apply your wrist power quickly.

THE QUICKER THE WRIST, THE MORE THE ROD LOADS, AND THE TIGHTER THE LOOP.

2.

The Loop And
Its Characteristics

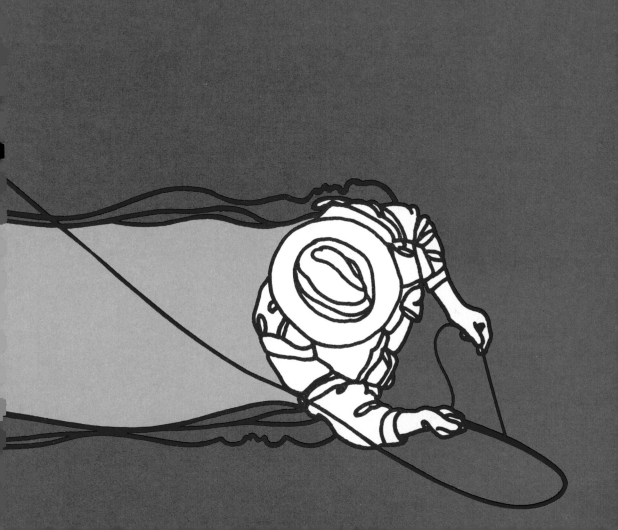

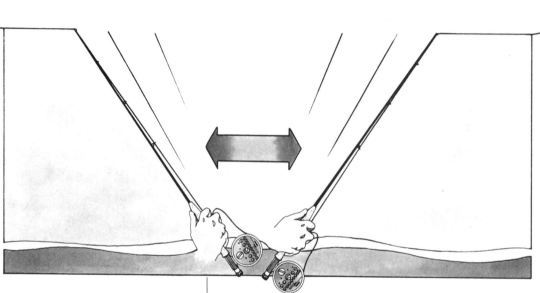

The Perfect loop.

2.1 The Loop

The **loop** is the configuration of the fly line after it rolls out from your rod tip. It is controlled by the movement of the rod tip, which, we have learned, is determined by the movement of the arm and wrist. Control of the loop's size, shape and direction is crucial to good, successful casting, because it really puts you in control of the presentation of your fly to the fish.

Counter Number

In visualizing the loop, think of a candy cane or the letter "J" placed on its side.

The loop is first formed by the back cast and then the opposite way as the front cast is thrown. The ability to regulate its size, shape, and direction is known as **"loop control."** Without this ability to control the loop's characteristics, you will never be more than just an average caster.

Notice the line as it rolls out from Doug's rod tip. You will notice that he has complete control of the loops he throws. It is critical that you develop this skill until it becomes automatic.

CONTROL OF THE LOOP REGULATES HOW YOU GET THE FLY TO THE FISH, AS WELL AS HOW THE FLY APPEARS TO THE FISH WHEN IT HITS THE WATER.

You will find yourself in many situations where loop control will make or break your successful presentation. For example, if you are fishing into the wind or under an overhead obstruction, you must throw a very tight loop.

THE KEY TO LOOP CONTROL IS IN CONTROLLING THE MOVEMENT AND SPEED OF THE ROD TIP.

2.2 Loop Size

The distance between the loop's top and bottom determines whether the loop is **"open"** or **"closed."** This distance is controlled by the movement of the rod tip. In most instances, a tighter loop is more desirable than a wide one because it has far less wind resistance, and is therefore far more efficient.

YOUR FLY LINE GOES WHERE THE ROD TIP DIRECTS IT.

In order to achieve a tight, efficient loop, you must develop a casting stroke that moves the rod tip in as straight a line as possible. If you apply the power of your wrist in a straight line directly at the target, the rod tip, and consequently the fly line, will follow.

THE STRAIGHTER AND FASTER THE TRAVEL OF THE ROD TIP, THE TIGHTER THE LOOP.

2.3 Loop Shape

Perfect loop shape, the ideal line configuration, is **a candy cane** with the top and bottom portions parallel and the front rounded. Most novice fly casters, however, throw either an Open or Closed Loop.

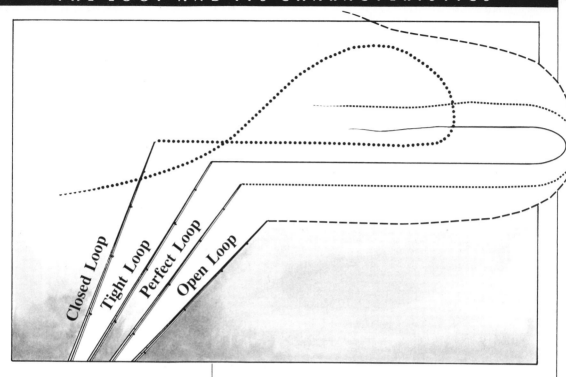

Closed Loop
Tight Loop
Perfect Loop
Open Loop

The Perfect Loop, The Open Loop, and The Closed, or Tailing Loop.

The perfect loop results when the front cast and back cast are lined up in a straight line, or 180 degrees apart. If you were to stretch a wire between two points in space, both front and back casts should lay on the wire.

The **Open Loop** is identified by the top portion of the candy cane angling up and away from the bottom portion. While the open loop will not foul or tangle into annoying ''wind knots,'' it will yield poor results in windy conditions because of its excessive wind resistance.

33

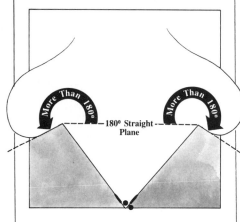

The Open Loop is thrown when the front and back cast are separated by more than 180 degrees. The Closed Loop is thrown when the front and back cast are separated by less than 180 degrees.

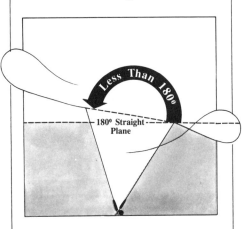

OPEN LOOPS ARE THROWN BECAUSE THE FRONT AND BACK CASTS ARE SEPARATED BY AN ANGLE GREATER THAN 180 DEGREES, OR MORE THAN A STRAIGHT LINE.

Likewise, the **Closed Loop,** or "Tailing" Loop, is a common occurrence. This loop shows the top portion of the candy cane angling down toward, and sometimes falling below, the bottom portion. This loop will often result in a tangled or fouled line and wind knots in your line.

Closed loops are thrown because the front and back casts are separated by an angle less than 180 degrees, or less than a straight line.

2.4 Loop Direction

The third loop characteristic is direction. Simply put, **loop direction** is where you aim your loops, both front and back. You can aim them high, low, right or left. Remember, this applies to *both* the front cast and back cast.

An extremely important rule evolves from the study of loop direction:

WHATEVER HAPPENS TO THE TIP OF YOUR LINE ON THE BACK CAST WILL BE REVERSED, OPPOSED EXACTLY 180 DEGREES, ON THE FRONT CAST.

If the tip of the line is low on the back cast, it will be high on the front cast. Conversely, if it is high on the back cast, it will come through low on the front cast. Likewise, when it is thrown to the right on the back cast, it reverses to the left on the front cast, and vice versa.

Understanding this simple but important concept will help you understand and correct many of your casting problems.

For example, if you are out on the stream and your fly keeps landing to the left of your target, you are undoubtedly throwing your back cast too far to the right. Likewise, if your fly keeps coming through low, hitting your rod tip or tangling in the leader, your back cast is probably too high.

THE BACK CAST AND THE FRONT CAST SHOULD BE IN DIRECT LINE WITH EACH OTHER, SEPARATED BY 180 DEGREES.

These two movements (back and front cast) must have a separation of 180 degrees, or **a "straight-line" relationship.** The perfect loop, with the top portion parallel to the bottom, is possible only when this straight-line relationship is created.

You should be sure that your front and back casts are in a perfectly straight line. Any casting plane can be used parallel to the water's surface, tilted up or tilted down, just as long as

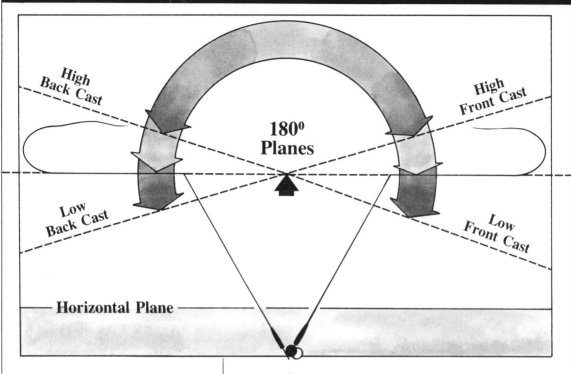

High Back Cast

180⁰ Planes

High Front Cast

Low Back Cast

Low Front Cast

Horizontal Plane

Vary the horizontal plane of your front and back cast, but be sure to separate them by 180 degrees.

both loops are thrown in a straight line. Concentrate on creating a smooth, straight-line flow of energy.

The key to loop control is in controlling your rod tip. You must control its movement and speed with your arm and wrist. It must move in a straight line so that your loops are well formed and efficient.

Watch how Doug casts, keeping his front and back casts on a flat plane, separated by 180 degrees. He is in control of the size, shape and direction of every loop he throws. Work hard to visualize these movements in your own mind, and then try them out on the practice field or on the water. Educate your muscles to duplicate Doug's movements. Compare your casting form to his, and practice until you can do it, too.

Next, as you are introduced to the basic casting stroke, you will learn to apply speed and power to loop control and the straight-line principle.

Action Steps For Loop Control

The best way to make this material your own is to do something with it. An armchair angler does not catch fish. It is only with practice that you will become a successful fly caster.

Complete the action steps after each chapter before trying to practice all of Doug's suggestions at once. Performing each skill separately will be the best way to commit these skills to your subconscious so that soon you will perform them instinctively.

The best way to develop systematically your skill is first to form an image in your mind of the movement you want to perform. Then, actually try that movement, to practice and perfect it. If your mental picture does not work, review the tape and the guidebook, and then repeat the process.

Comprehension and proper application of the straight-line principle, combined with control of the loops you throw, will put you in complete command of even the most difficult casting situations. By regularly practicing these action steps, you will see rapid improvement in your strength, accuracy and confidence.

1. Using your fly rod or yarn rod, practice watching both your back cast and your front cast. Develop the habit of always turning your neck back and forth on every casting stroke so that watching both movements becomes an automatic part of your training.

2. Imagine that you are painting a straight line with your rod tip. Beginners sometimes pick up this concept more quickly by casting sidearm, or in the horizontal plane. Stand facing a sidewalk, or other straight line on the ground, and make the rod tip follow the line during the casting stroke. Once the stroke is mastered in the horizontal plane, slowly elevate to a more vertical plane, where such things as telephone wires and roof lines can be used as guides for painting straight strokes. Also, indoors, use your yarn rod to trace straight lines on the ceiling.

3. On the practice field, try throwing various loop shapes, carefully watching both your back cast and your front cast. Make sure that your rod tip is traveling in a perfectly straight line. Start with tight and wide loops, throwing several of each and then mixing up the sequence. Shout out such commands as

"Wide loop front," "Tight loop rear," "Tight loop front," "Wide loop rear," and then immediately perform those movements. Every loop should form a stop-action image in your mind as you do it and should then be reviewed. Ask yourself if your arm and wrist did what your mind told them to do. In this manner, timing can be refined.

4. Practice control of your loop in every plane - sidearm, straight up, backhanded, and everything in between. Keep the loop tight, but not closed, and keep your thumb in the same position for every casting angle. Use varying lengths of line, from 15 to 40 feet.

5. Line up the front and back casting planes. Not only should your front and back loops be lined up straight when observed from the side or ground level, but they should also be in a straight line when viewed from above, as from an airplane. The feel of proper alignment can be learned quickly by standing next to a curb, edge of a driveway, or any straight line, and making sure both the front and back loops stay directly over the line.

Practicing these exercises regularly will enable you to automatically pre-form the loop configuration that is most appropriate for any situation that you face.

COMING UP NEXT: THE BASIC
CASTING STROKE

3.

The Basic
Casting Stroke

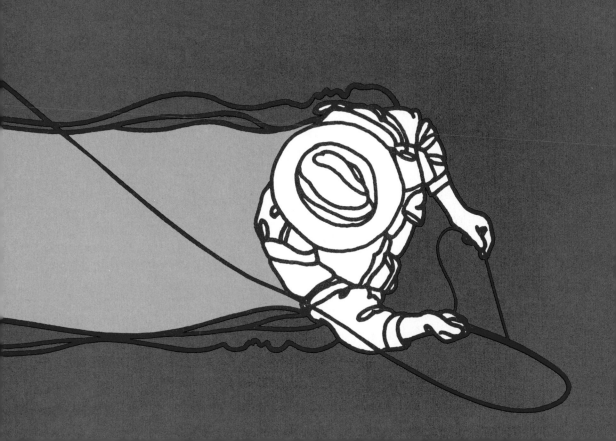

3.1 Basic Casting Stroke

The **basic casting stroke** is the foundation for any and every cast. Though the basic stroke is uncomplicated, it is crucial that you learn it well. Up to this point, you have been training your mind to visualize the elements of the cast, such as loop control or straight-line energy transfer. Now, with the basic casting stroke, you will begin to train your muscles to combine these elements perfectly.

The basic casting stroke, in addition to comprising the skills you have seen so far, is possible only by blending the proper grip and stance with controlled arm and wrist movements.

Mastery of the basic stroke is the key to becoming a successful fly fisherman, and is necessary before tackling any of the presentation casts.

THE BASIC CASTING STROKE IS THE FOUNDATION FOR ALL PRESENTATION CASTS.

3.2 Grip

Before attempting the basic casting stroke, you must first learn **a proper grip.** The most practical and efficient grip is where the thumb is on

Counter Number

the top of the handle, opposite the reel. It is similar to the grip that you use when picking up a suitcase and should be loose and relaxed.

More power and control can be delivered with this grip than with any other. By keeping your thumb on top of the rod, you are automatically restricted from letting your rod tip go back too far, therefore dropping out of a straight line. It also allows you to apply maximum energy directly to the target.

3.3 Stance

The correct stance is important to the development of good casting technique. While practicing, it is best to stand at a slight angle so that you can look easily back over your casting shoulder to keep an eye on the back cast. You cannot improve your cast without being able to see it.

When fishing in the stream, your stance should allow you to face your target directly, but don't forget about throwing a good back cast. In fact, even when fishing, Doug turns his head every few minutes or so to check his back cast.

Note that Doug's body movements are smooth and fluid, not stiff. Even though he is alert and ready for anything to happen on the water, he keeps a relaxed body attitude.

3.4 Arm Movement

When performing the basic casting stroke, use your arm to set up the power stroke of the wrist.

To help you visualize the arm movement that is necessary for the basic casting stroke, imagine yourself standing in a doorway, facing one of the jambs. With a double-headed hammer, drive a nail horizontally into the front jamb with the forestroke and another nail into the opposite jamb with the back stroke. The nails should be exactly 180 degrees apart and at shoulder level.

In order to hit the nails squarely, you will quickly find that the hammer and wrist must stay in a "cocked" position until the very end of the stroke.

This motion is very similar to the basic casting stroke. Long, straight-line, pushing and pulling movements are combined with a quick, powerful wrist movement.

3.5 The "Micro-Second Wrist"

The snap of the wrist is a "micro" part of the total casting stroke. It takes only a "micro-second." The "micro-second wrist" is one of the key factors to Doug Swisher's casting technique. Developing your micro-second wrist, along with the basic casting stroke, will result in your building the basis for perfect fly presentation.

The speed of this quick wrist movement loads the rod more, adds velocity to the line, and gives the cast its power. Increased line velocity, combined with loop control, enables you to counteract wind and cast further.

To educate your wrist, you must learn to control the amount of arc that you put into your wrist snap. It is possible, with practice, to apply great wrist power to your cast by using a very narrow arc.

TRAIN YOUR WRIST TO SNAP IN AS STRAIGHT A LINE AS POSSIBLE. REMEMBER: TRAIN YOUR MIND TO "SEE" IT, AND THEN TRAIN YOUR MUSCLES TO "DO" IT.

The arc that the wrist creates, from point A to point B, should be no more than 90 degrees. Think of this angle as "a piece of pie." Just like at the dinner table, avoid cutting too large a piece. The 90 degree arc is not an exact standard, especially for the advanced caster, but is a good guideline for the beginner.

A 90 degree arc, executed in a flat plane, will result in a well-formed, tight loop. More than a 90 degree arc will give you a wide, wind resistant loop, and an arc that is significantly less

A. *Extend the casting hand a full arm's length in the casting direction, keeping the hand at shoulder level;*

B. *Now pull the rod in a straight line toward your shoulder, keeping the rod aimed forward at approximately 45 degrees.*

C. *When your hand is about even with your ear, snap the rod back through no more than a 90 degree arc, with a smooth, super-quick motion of the wrist.*

D. After a brief pause, until
   the line is almost straight
   behind you, reverse the
   procedure by pushing the
   rod forward, keeping it
   aimed back about 45
   degrees.

E. When the arm is almost
   fully extended, snap the
   rod forward, back to the
   starting point.

than 90 degrees will be closed and likely to foul.

Give it a try. Having set your grip, extend the casting hand a full arm's length in the direction of the cast, keeping the hand at shoulder level, thumb on top of the cork, and the rod butt aimed forward about 45 degrees. From this starting position, you will initiate the back cast.

Now, pull the rod toward your shoulder in a perfectly straight line, with your arm parallel to the ground, keeping the rod tip aimed forward about 45 degrees. This is a slow, deliberate movement. When your hand is about even with your ear, snap the rod quickly but smoothly back through no more than a 90 degree arc. Do not have the rod aimed more than 45 degrees to the rear. This completes the back cast.

After a brief pause, reverse the procedure by pushing the rod straight forward, keeping it aimed back about 45 degrees. This is also a slow, deliberate movement.

When the arm is almost fully extended, snap the rod forward quickly and smoothly, again through no more than a 90 degree arc, back to the starting point. This completes the basic casting stroke.

During the push and pull portions of the basic casting stroke, the beginning caster should maintain the 45 degree position - 45 degrees forward during the back cast, and 45 degrees backward during the front cast, as it will help in learning the last-second snap of the wrist. One of the biggest mistakes made by the beginner is snapping the wrist too soon. On the other hand, the advanced caster will allow the rod to start drifting, or changing its arc, during the push and pull movements. This produces a smoother casting stroke and helps to eliminate tailing loops.

Also, most beginners tend to have too little snap in their stroke. Don't be too timid. Doug is applying his wrist snap so quickly that it doesn't look like much of a snap at all; that is why it's called the "micro-second" wrist. Most beginners do not get the feel of the casting until they get the snap. Develop a powerful snap in the beginning, and then begin to work on its smoothness.

You will find that more than any other element, the secret of successful fly casting is a quick, well-educated wrist.

THE ARM SETS UP THE BASIC CASTING STROKE, AND THE WRIST IS THE POWER.

As you try this stroke in faster motion, you will see that the challenge of the basic casting stroke is in blending a fluid "push-pull" movement of the arm, with the dynamic power application of the wrist.

By working on the separate movements individually, you will find that the entire stroke will take on an increased fluidness. Through practice, you will add timing and strength to your technique. You are then on your way to becoming an accomplished caster. As you gain mastery of this basic movement, you will find that you rely less on your arm movement, and are primarily casting with just your wrist.

Watch Doug execute the basic casting stroke on the videotape, study the drawings, and visualize it in your head. Then, go out onto the practice field to train your muscles to do exactly what your "mind's eye" sees.

Action Steps For Perfecting The Basic Casting Stroke

In the transition from practice field to actual stream conditions, everyone's technique changes at least a little bit. Your thinking is focused less on your style, and more on your actual fishing action. This is why you should take the time to perfect your technique on the practice field, and not on the stream, wasting valuable fishing time.

1. On the practice field, lay 20 feet of line straight on the grass. Try the basic casting stroke, front and back. If your line tangles,

try "half strokes" - just one back cast and then one front cast at a time. Stop your casting motion after either one front or one back cast, and let the line lay out on the ground before you perform the motion in the opposite direction.

Emphasize the movement of your wrist, but don't squeeze the rod. Hold it loosely, and above all, stay relaxed. Don't reach too high or too low. Practice on a comfortable level with your hand at about ear height.

2. Review the loop control exercise. Add the "plane and tilt" exercise, to be able to cast in every plane, and handle every angle (tilt, down, straight ahead and high). To help develop a tight loop, practice snapping your wrist as quickly as possible, keeping the rod tip traveling in a straight line. Allow no more than a 90 degree arc movement of the rod.

3. Use these visual checks:

   A. "The piece of pie." Check the angle your rod creates during each cast. It should be no more than 90 degrees. You need a 90 degree or less arc for a well-formed, tight loop. A wider arc will result in too wide a loop. If the "piece of pie" is too narrow, the loop may tangle. Keep it at 90 degrees maximum.

B. Be sure that your wrist moves fast and straight, on a flat plane. Try not to twist your wrist.

C. Observe your rod tip. Is it in a straight-line path? Watch your line in the air on both the front and back casts. Trace straight lines such as telephone wires and roof lines.

4. Doug endorses monitoring your "noise factor" as another check. If you are working too hard to get the line out, you will be able to hear the noise created as the rod is pushed through the air. A proper cast will make little or no noise. Very little effort is required. So, if you can hear your line distinctly, reduce your power. By doing this, and practicing your casting timing regularly, you won't work harder than you have to.

5. Any of these exercises can be done to music. Because casting is so centered around the timing of a series of movements, music and steady rhythm are an ideal accompaniment.

COMING UP NEXT:
PRESENTATION CASTS

4.

Presentation Casts and Techniques

Now you are geared up and ready to go after the challenge of mastering your first presentation cast, the straight line cast. If you need work on any particular element of the basic casting stroke, this is where it will show up.

4.2 The Straight-Line Cast

THE STRAIGHT LINE CAST IS THE BASIC BUILDING BLOCK FOR ALL OTHER CASTS.

It is a "low-profile" cast. Aim it low over the water, so that the cast will be unaffected by wind and misdirection. **The straight line cast** should have a tight loop, so that there is a minimum of wind resistance to keep it from making a straight, direct path to the target.

Aim is critical. Even a super-tight loop won't straighten out if it is aimed over the horizon. It will sail like an airplane wing, and fall back to the water in a series of sine waves. If you aim too low, you'll fall short of the target.

Remember to keep the loop tight, in a straight, direct line toward the target.

Notice how Doug achieves a smooth, straight presentation of his fly by casting on an angle just below the horizon, and lowers the rod at the end of his cast. This gives him a more

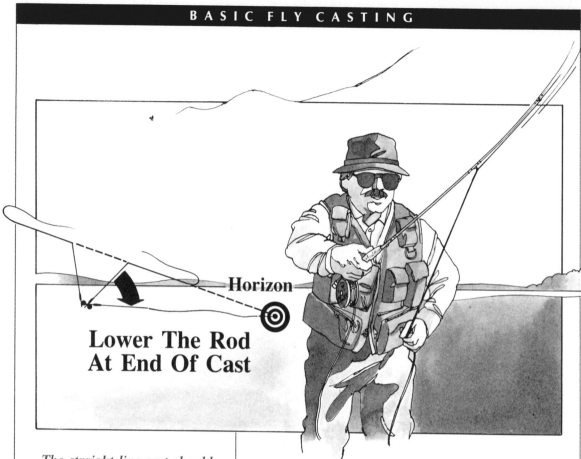

Horizon

Lower The Rod At End Of Cast

The straight line cast should have a tight loop, and a low and direct profile.

delicate presentation, and puts the rod in proper fishing position for setting hooks and controlling slack line.

The straight line cast is the basic cast for fishing dry flies upstream as well as most wet flies in streams and stillwater. It is the cast you will use most often in lakes and when fishing streamers. All other casts evolve from the straight line cast.

4.3 The Pick-Up and Lay-Down Cast

With **the pick-up and lay-down cast,** only one back cast is made. This technique increases your efficiency on the water by reducing the false casting time and increasing your fishing time.

It is critical to get your fly line straight before you make the back cast. To get the line totally straight, the rod tip should be right on the water, and all the slack should be stripped in. A high rod angle puts a bow in the line, thus creating too much slack to load the rod. Also, extend the casting arm. This gives more room for the pulling part of the pick-up and allows for a smoother, more efficient back cast.

Notice Doug's casting thumb is parallel to the water at the beginning of the pick-up, and is perpendicular to the water at the end of the back cast. This is the 90 degree piece of pie that is so important and ensures a high back cast. As soon as the line straightens to the rear, drive the front cast directly to the target.

4.4 Changing Direction With a Minimum of False Casting

There are many occasions where your pick-up must be made in one direction and your lay-down, or delivery, must be made in another direction. For these situations, you will want to use a change of direction cast.

This cast is especially helpful when fishing across stream. Normally with this type of fishing, you will cast 45 degrees upstream and then let your fly drift to a position 45 degrees downstream, covering what Doug calls "The Cross-Stream Quadrant."

At the end of the drift, to go back to the target 90 degrees upstream, change direction while you false cast. Notice that in order to change direction 90 degrees, Doug uses three false casts of 30 degrees each, or two false casts of 45 degrees each.

Eventually, with practice, you can change direction the full 90 degrees without false casting.

4.5 Shooting Line

Shooting allows you to reach out and cover more water without moving closer to your target. This saves you precious time and gives you a wider casting range for when you cannot get any closer to your target.

This is accomplished by releasing the line on the front cast. Through the combined momentum of back and forth false casting, and micro-second power stroke, additional line is shot through your guides at the end of the cast.

Notice Doug's timing. Timing is critical to shooting line. The wrist snap is made just after the loop has begun traveling to the target. If your line shoots way up in the air, you are letting go too soon.

With a little practice, a tight loop, and good wrist timing, you can easily extend your casting range.

On the practice field, it is OK to let go of the line when you shoot, but when you are fishing, keep contact with the line by letting it slide through your fingers. Form an ''O-ring'' with your thumb and index finger. This puts you in the position of always having control of the line. This is important when you are fishing.

When shooting line, most fly casters make the mistake of totally changing their technique on their final forward cast. They false cast beautifully, throwing tight, well shaped loops back and forth, but then, instead of maintaining the same efficient loop for the shooting cast, they try to add extra power and end up with a loop that is two to three times bigger than the false cast. In an effort to add the extra power, they let their rod tip drop too far out of a straight line, thus opening the loop, which, of course, greatly increases the wind resistance and dissipates power in too many directions.

The solution to this problem is to false cast right at your target, being careful not to aim too high, and then just let it go. This way there is no room to change your technique. This is one of the biggest problems with beginning casters. They false cast too high, and then have to change direction too much on their delivery cast.

Note how Doug aims low, tight at the target, and does not change his technique when he shoots. Notice also how Doug strips line off of his reel, and coils it in his left hand, to keep it off the water. He shoots some of this line on his false cast, and then shoots the rest on his final delivery cast.

4.6 The Control System

This is a system of controlling the line once the cast is made.

YOU MUST STAY IN CONTROL OF YOUR LINE ONCE IT HITS THE WATER.

It is extremely important to know how to do this, because without **line control,** you cannot take in slack, set the hook, or make smooth, efficient pickups. It also makes your fishing

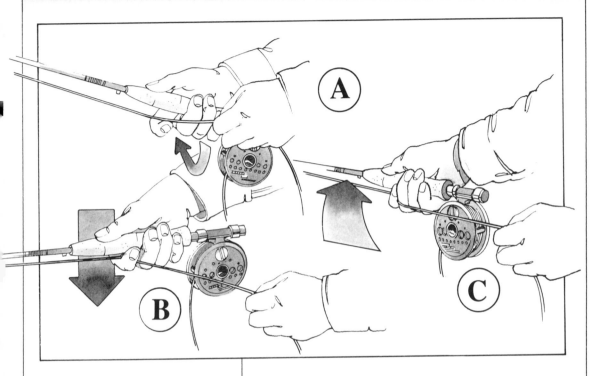

The three steps of The Control System:

A. Put the line over the finger.

B. Lower the rod tip to the water.

C. Follow the drifting line with the rod tip. Stay in control of your line so that you can control slack, set hooks, and make smooth pickups.

time more effective by giving you longer, drag-free floats.

These are Doug's three steps to line control:

1. Put the line over your finger as soon as your cast is made. If you do not put the line over your finger, you cannot effectively control the slack in your system. You can neither strip line in, nor let line out. Putting the line over your finger is the ideal position for maintaining control of the line while stripping.

2. Lower the rod tip to the water. If you do not, drag will set into your fly line almost immediately. You are also in a bad position for setting a hook or making the pick-up for the next cast.

3. Follow the drift of the fly line on the water with your rod tip. Your rod tip, pointed at the fly, must move in sync with the fly at the speed of the current to prevent drag.

This control system is yet another application of the straight line principle *after* the cast has been made. Direct, straight lines to the target, as long as drag does not set in, make you an efficient fisherman.

Master this system, and you will be able to control your line in any situation. You will miss fewer strikes and have longer, more efficient drifts.

Combining the straight-line system with shooting and the control system provides all the techniques necessary to go to your favorite water and enjoy putting what you have learned into practice.

4.7 The Slack Line Cast

The slack line cast is just as important to the dry fly or nymph fisherman as the straight-line cast is to the streamer or stillwater angler.

In lakes and ponds, or when fishing streamers, it is important to be able to throw a cast that lands perfectly straight, not only because more water can be covered, but, more importantly, because the retrieval of the fly begins instantly.

However, for the stream fisherman who must present his dry flies and nymphs in a drag-free manner, the slack line cast is necessary. It is an excellent way to achieve a natural float when casting across stream currents of various speeds. By putting slack between you and your fly, you get a much longer drag-free drift than you would get with a straight-line cast.

Using more line than is required to reach the target is the key to making effective drag-free presentation. By distributing excess line in a series of sine waves, or "wrinkles," between you and your target, you are "buying time," and longer drag-free floats.

The straight line cast, because there is no slack between you and the fly, can only provide the *briefest* drag-free float at best.

Notice how Doug aims his front loop high over the horizon and quickly drops the rod tip to the water. This causes the line to land on the water in a sine wave configuration, creating slack line between the rod tip and the target.

Use of the wide loop on the delivery cast is a prime example of how to apply "loop knowledge'' in solving a stream problem. Loop separation in this cast is less than 180 degrees (a high front cast with a horizontal back cast), and will result in closing loops, so you must keep them wide, to prevent tangling.

More sine waves mean more slack, and with more slack you are gaining more drag-free drift time. More drag-free drift time means your fly will behave in a natural manner longer, thus increasing the time during which a trout is likely to take your fly.

Don't worry that you will not be able to set hooks when using the slack line cast. Just keep the line as tight as you can without dragging the fly, and a gentle lifting of the arm will do the trick.

A straight line cast, especially one made across current lanes of varying speeds, can only provide a very brief natural drift. A slack line cast made to the same target will increase your natural drift time manyfold. Mastering it is a major step toward being able to *catch trout that others can't.*

Combining all of the techniques that you have seen so far makes a great system and provides you with the versatility and flexibility needed to adapt to many situations. These are the keys to mastery of the sport. You will be introduced to many more useful combinations of presentation and line control techniques in the next tape in this series, "Advanced Fly Casting."

Action Steps For Presentation Casts And Techniques

1. Cast loops using only your wrist, and then some using only your arm. To produce straight-line rod tip travel with your wrist, a super-quick power application must be used. Notice how the rod must be snapped in a very small arc in order to throw a tight loop. Your timing must be perfect to execute a perfect loop.

   Now throw some loops with only your arm, using a push-pull motion to make the rod tip travel in a straight line. Notice that the wrist provides acceleration and power while the arm smoothes out the loops and keeps the line from fouling.

2. Isometrics. You will find that once you have become proficient at loop control, strength becomes a big factor. Using a wooden dowel, or the butt end of an old rod, simulate casting positions, both front and back, by applying pressure to the dowel as you hold it against a stationary surface for about ten seconds. Hold the end of the dowel or butt section in a doorway, in the corner of a room or on a tree limb. Just two or three minutes a day will greatly increase the strength of your arm, wrist and hand.

3. Hang a hula hoop from a tree limb, or some other support. Line up the center of the loop to be about head level, and try to throw your front loop through it without hitting the edges. When you consistently make your front cast go through without fouling, then work on your back cast. This practice will quickly reduce the size of your loops so you can easily cast into tight, difficult areas on the stream, such as underneath overhanging tree limbs and bushes. With practice, you will be able to fish spots that others cannot.

4. Work on these shooting exercises to help you cover more water with less effort:

   A. The long shoot: This is where you get your false cast moving back and forth, then shoot the line forward as far as you can. This is a great method of improving your basic casting stroke and general efficiency on the stream.

   B. The short shoot: The wrist is always a key factor with shooting, but especially with this exercise. Your wrist should provide virtually all the power here. Throw a high back cast, and snap it forward with the wrist. This exercise is considerably more difficult because only one rod length of line is used, and since there is less line mass to help load the rod, you must load it with your quick wrist. The short shoot is the best way to develop a micro-second wrist. It is especially useful also because it closely simulates common fishing situations. As you progress with this exercise, see if you can do it using a double rod length of line.

C. The back shoot: After you have perfected forward shooting, try shooting line on your back cast. You should be able to shoot backward as far as you do forward. Remember, a good back cast makes a good front cast. Mastery of this exercise will greatly improve your entire casting technique.

There are two ways to practice the back shoot. You can either false cast and let it go, as Doug shows in the videotape, or you can simply pick the line up right off the grass in front of you and shoot it to the rear with a single stroke.

5. Tailing, or tangling, loops are caused by the rod being in the wrong position or forming the wrong "piece of pie" during the power stroke. The problem is in starting the snap of the wrist too soon, which, of course, means that the rod is tipped back too far when the front power stroke is started and tipped forward too far when the backcast power stroke is initiated. To correct this problem, practice "holding off" with the wrist snap until the

rod passes the 12 o'clock (vertical) position in each direction.

Congratulations on completing this program! But do not stop here! Now, it is time to put all that you have learned to use. If you have been completing the action steps at the end of each chapter, it will be easier now to integrate all of your new knowledge and skills. Still, when you actually go out to fish, so much is happening that it is easy to become overwhelmed.

Be patient. You will make the most progress (and be able to see that progress) if you prepare for each trip and then take the time afterwards to reflect on your successes, problems, and future challenges.

Make this video guidebook material "your own." Review this program again and again -- actually several times within the next few months. (60% to 70% of everything you hear only once is forgotten within 24 hours.) Refer to the videotape, so that Doug's examples help you to visualize in your own mind exactly how you should be performing the steps you have learned. First train your mind, and then train your muscles.

You'll become the kind of angler you want to be when the concepts and skills presented in this program are second nature to you. GOOD LUCK!

TO BUILD ON YOUR BASIC FOUNDATION OF CASTING SKILLS AND TECHNIQUES, AND BECOME THE BEST THAT YOU CAN BE, VIEW DOUG'S NEXT TAPE IN THIS SERIES "ADVANCED FLY CASTING."

Appendix

Glossary

All sports, professions and pursuits have developed their own language. Fly fishing is no exception. Part of the enjoyment of the sport is mastering the language.

Backing

The line that goes *on* the reel first -- under the fly line itself. It's basically an insurance policy against losing a big fish that goes on a long run. For trout fishing, the backing consists of fifty yards of twenty-pound test braided dacron casting line. Many anglers, once they've spooled the fly line on over the backing, never see it again until they change fly lines. If you're one of them, this Mastery Series can move you into the ''I got taken into my backing'' category.

Current Lanes

Lanes in a stream refer to a specific route being taken by any part of the water coming downstream. For example, when water hits a rock, some of it usually goes around one side and some around the other -- those are two different current lanes.

Delivery Cast

This is the final casting stroke that actually places your fly on the water. It is the deciding factor of good or bad presentation.

False Casting	All the casting, back and forth, that goes on in the air without the fly or fly line touching the water is called false casting. It is either done to dry the fly, lengthen the line, or change casting direction.
Flat Water	Go look at a slow moving stream with virtually no rocks or obstructions on the bottom. How does it look compared to the choppy, turbulent surface of a fast moving stream with lots of subsurface obstructions? Flat, right? In addition to a flat surface, flat water also means a relatively slow current.
Fly	"Fly" in its general use means an imitation insect, tied on a hook, at the end of the tippet (which is at the end of the leader, which is at the end of the fly line, and so on, and so on). When fly fisherman speak of "dry flies," however, they are referring to the ones that float on the surface (most of the time). If they speak of "wet flies," they mean those which are fished under the surface or "nymphs" (which imitate the immature nymphal stage of aquatic insects that live on the bottom of the stream). Streamers are designed to imitate baitfish, and are a type of "wet fly."
Fly Drag	A situation when the fly is moving faster or slower than the water it is floating on. This is usually caused by the line or leader floating on a lane of water current that is moving at a different speed than the lane of water the fly is on.

This means that the fly is "dragged" along as the faster or slower current lane pulls on the line or leader, and therefore, the fly no longer drifts at the speed a free-floating insect would. In other words, a dragging fly gives an unnatural surface impression, and the trout refuse to strike. You will notice in this videotape that Doug continually stresses the importance of avoiding fly drag.

Fly Fishing Vest

Sometimes referred to as a "walking tackle shop." Doug carries plenty of equipment, but he's learned how to organize it. His vest is like a filing system -- a place for everything and everything in its place.

Fly Floatant

A paste or liquid dressing that is put on *dry* flies. In fast water, floatant is also applied to the tippet so it won't get waterlogged and sink.

Fly Rod

Line weight determines what rod is appropriate to a given situation. You decide what line weight fits the situation, then use a rod built to cast that weight line. Rods can usually tolerate about one weight size above or below the weight size they are built for. They will not cast well with lines that are much lighter or heavier. One or two rods will not cover all the situations you will ever fish -- unless you stick to only one basic type of water. This has to be one of the great all-time excuses to buy another, and yet another, rod.

Leader	The piece of monofilament line between the fly line and the fly. For dry fly fishing, the total length of the leader is usually a minimum of 7-½ feet and a maximum of 12 to 15 feet.
Lie	Where fish ''lie in wait'' (for something to eat or for danger to pass). Also referred to as ''location.''
Load	''Loading the rod'' is storing energy in it, not unlike pulling on a bow.
Loop	The loop is the configuration of the fly line during the cast as it rolls out from your rod tip. Control of its size, shape and direction is crucial to good presentation and successful casting.
Pockets	Areas of smooth, slower water behind current obstructions (usually rocks) in streams or rivers. Pockets are good fish-holding areas.
Pools	Deep areas in rivers where the current is slow. Pools usually occur at the end of a riffle, rapid or waterfall, where the current has dug out the river bottom. They also occur where the terrain has allowed the stream to widen, and, as a consequence, the current is slower. Pools are fish-holding areas.
Presentation	Technically speaking, presentation is not just casting. It is also the other part of technique. Casting gets the fly to the general area. Presentation is what goes on just before and after it

lands. Specifically, the term comes from ''presenting'' the fly to the fish. What does the fly look like? Does it look ''real'' to the fish? How does it move? For example, a fly dragging across the surface when the insect that it is supposed to imitate is drifting motionless with the current, is the result of a poor presentation. Good presentation means the fly looks and acts as natural as possible.

Throughout this guidebook and the entire Mastery Series, we treat the whole issue of getting the fly to the fish as ''presentation.''

Seam

A seam is the point where two current lanes of different speeds meet. Achieving a long, drag-free float when casting across a seam or seams of current is one of the fly caster's greatest challenges.

Sine Waves

When you throw a proper slack line cast, your line should fall on the water in a curved, or serpentine pattern. The curves in your line are described as a series of ''sine waves.''

Sunglasses

Other than having the right rod, reel, line, leader, tippet and fly for the situation, Doug would probably give up anything before he'd give up a good pair of *polarized* sunglasses. The reason is that with them, you can see fish; without them, you hardly ever can.

Tippet

The end portion of the leader. The piece of small diameter monofilament the fly is actually tied to. May be 2 to 5 feet long.

Wind Knots

If you throw a closed loop, have bad timing, cast into heavy winds, or have poor technique in general, you run a sizeable risk of having your line foul or tangle into "wind knots."

For more information about other fine Fly Fishing products, contact these companies for their catalogs:

Columbia Sportswear
6600 North Baltimore
P.O. Box 03239
Portland, Oregon 97203

Sage
9630 N.E. Lafayette Street
Bainbridge Island, Washington 98110

Scientific Anglers
Bldg. 223 3S
3M Center
St. Paul, MN 55144-1000

Simms Products Division
Life-Link International, Inc.
1240 Huff Lane
Jackson Hole, Wyoming 83001

A special "Thank You" is extended to all those who contributed to this Mastery Learning System.

Admark Group

Babcock & Schmid Associates

Bob Bakken Graphic Designer

Doug Swisher

Carmichael Lynch

Growth Resources Group

Halloran and Associates

Marjorie Nuggent

Bob Prasciunas Illustrator

R.R. Donnelley and Sons

Seitz Yamamoto Moss

For More Information Write To:
Scientific Anglers
Bldg. 223-3S
3M Center
St. Paul, Minnesota 55144-1000

Notes

Notes

Notes

Notes

Notes

Notes

Notes

Notes

Notes

Notes

Notes

For More Information Write To:
Scientific Anglers
Bldg. 223-3S
3M Center
St. Paul, Minnesota 55144-1000

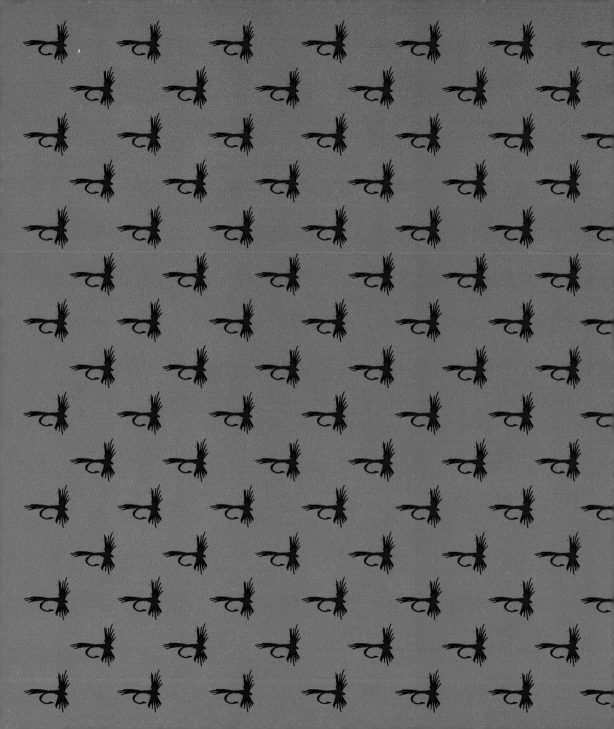

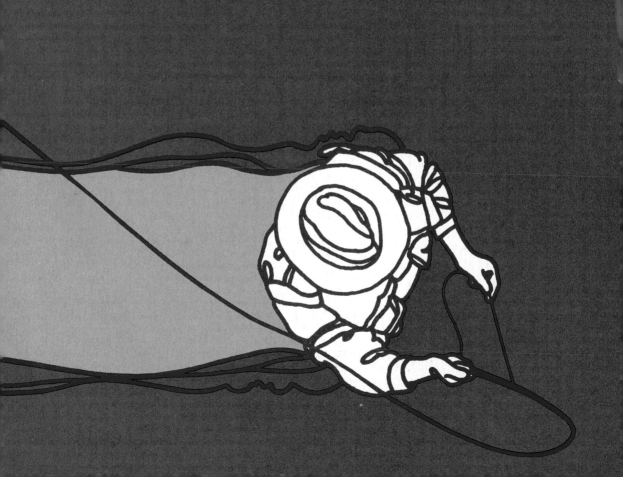

4.1 Presentation Cast

Here is where you get to put it all together. The following presentation casts integrate everything that you have seen so far.

Before we go any further, let's take a look at some of the equipment that Doug is using:

Your rod should be lightweight but powerful, and should have a crisp action. The Sage Graphite II rod that Doug is using makes it very easy for him to throw tight loops.

His vest, made by Columbia, is his portable tackle shop and meets his need for organization while fishing. He knows where everything is located in its large, convenient pockets.

Doug's reel, a System I (model 456), is made by Scientific Anglers. Doug chose this reel because it's lightweight, well-balanced, and has a smooth, dependable drag system.

His line is also made by Scientific Anglers. You will find, as Doug does, that the SA line is a pleasure to fish with.

Finally, his waders are made by Simms. They are made of flexible, form-fitting Neoprene rubber which stretches when you do. They'll keep you warm on the coldest of opening days.

Counter Number